LUMINOUS BODIES
CIRCLES OF CELEBRATION

MELINDA CAMBER PORTER ARCHIVE
OF
CREATIVE WORKS
Volume 2, Number 2

LUMINOUS BODIES
CIRCLES OF CELEBRATION

BY
MELINDA CAMBER PORTER

FOREWORD BY
PETER TRIPPI

Blake Press

Published by Blake Press

© 2016 Blake Press
© 2016 MELINDA CAMBER PORTER ARCHIVE

Library of Congress Control Number: 2015908050
  Camber Porter, Melinda
  Luminous Bodies: Circles of Celebration
  Camber Porter, Melinda
  Watercolors, Drawings, Illustrations and Poetry
  Lannon, Frances
  Luminous Bodies: Circles of Celebration
  Trippi, Peter
  Luminous Bodies: Circles of Celebration

ISBN 978-1-942231-49-3
  1.   Blake, William—Art, Poetry and Spiritualism.
  2.   Camber Porter, Melinda—Criticism and interpretation.
  3.   Camber Porter, Melinda—Watercolors and Drawings.
  4.   Camber Porter, Melinda—Art, Poetry and Spiritualism.
  5.   Drawings, literature, and poetry—English.
  6.   Illuminated works—Great Britain.
  7.   Lannon, Frances—Criticism and Interpretation.
  8.   Tibetan Book of the Dead—Death, Life, and Spiritualism.
  9.   Trippi, Peter—Criticism and interpretation.

Melinda Camber Porter Archive of Creative Works:
Series in Art and Literature: Volume 2, Number 2
  ISSN: 2379-2450 (Print)
  ISSN: 2379-3198 (EBook - Online)
  ISSN: 2370-321X (Audiobook)

Editor: Joseph R. Flicek

First Edition POD

www.MelindaCamberPorter.com

Frontispiece:
A Circle of Celebration, n.d.
Hand-engraved block print on Himalayan handmade Lokta paper
Artist Unknown

MELINDA CAMBER PORTER ARCHIVE
OF
CREATIVE WORKS

The Melinda Camber Porter Archive of Creative Works comprises two series of books. The First Series are books of journalism. The Second Series are books of art and literature.

Publisher's Note

Dr. Frances Lannon, Principal of Lady Margaret Hall of Oxford University, provides us with her opening remarks at the time of Luminous Bodies Exhibition in 2004 held in the Jerwood Gallery, Lady Margaret Hall. Dr. Lannon states, "We are particularly pleased to show Melinda Camber Porter's art, because she is herself a former student of Lady Margaret Hall, and this exhibition represents in a very direct way the College's ongoing commitment to the visual arts."

Peter Trippi, an art historian and editor of *Fine Art Connoisseur*, who gave several joint lectures with Melinda Camber Porter before her death, states in his Foreword, "In an era of slickly produced images, teeming with messages rather than feelings, Melinda Camber Porter's pictures strike a distinctive balance between the achingly personal and the aesthetically beautiful."

Melinda Camber Porter introduces the reader to the *Luminous Bodies Series* by stating it is "a work of mourning and an exploration of the spiritual and cultural forces that continuously vie to originate and then heal the rift between the body and the soul. Inspired by many religious traditions of mourning, from *The Tibetan Book of the Dead* to Native American mourning rituals, the series of drawings is, in actuality, a spiritual journey begun by the artist a few days after the death of a loved one. The journey is narrated in drawings and in epigrammatic prose poetry inscribed within the images."

The Luminous Bodies Series consists of ninety watercolors chosen from over 200 watercolors by Melinda Camber Porter and she placed them in six circles of "Celebration and Mourning." Peter Trippi describes this as Camber Porter's "own Cosmology" or a spiritual journey of the living and the dead with rebirths. Luminous Bodies Series is published in two volumes of forty-five watercolors in each.

Circles of Celebration comprises the first volume of *Luminous Bodies*.

TABLE OF CONTENTS

LIST OF PLATES

OPENING REMARKS
FROM JERWOOD GALLERY
BY DR. FRANCES LANNON

It was a great pleasure for me to welcome all those who attended the opening and private view of an exhibition of paintings from Melinda Camber Porter's series *Luminous Bodies* at Lady Margaret Hall (LMH), Oxford, on 2 November 2004. I am delighted now to have the opportunity of welcoming viewers and readers to this volume, which brings together Melinda's paintings and the fascinating and instructive talk that Robin Hamlyn [Vol. II, No.3] gave on that occasion.

The exhibition was one of a wonderful Jerwood series that LMH was privileged to host from 2000 to 2005. The aim of the organiser, Dr. Allan Doig (Keeper of Pictures at LMH), was to present current work by contemporary artists working in different media, including oils, watercolours, drawings, photography, installation, and digital. We are enormously grateful to the Jerwood Foundation for its generous sponsorship of this series. In many cases, the private view began with a talk about the paintings or about a subject that illuminated them. Artists in the series included Maggi Hambling, Anya Gallaccio, John Maddison,

and Roger Wagner. Speakers included Marina Warner, Griselda Pollock, and Dame Gillian Weir. Robin Hamlyn's talk, and Melinda Camber Porter's paintings, made a distinctive and powerful contribution to the series.

Robin Hamlyn is Senior Curator and Head of Collections for the period 1780–1860 at the Tate. He is an authority on William Blake. He is the author, with Michael Philips, of William Blake, published by the Tate Trustees in 2000 to accompany a major exhibition of Blake's work at Tate Britain in London and the Metropolitan Museum of Art in New York. Melinda Camber Porter is a painter and writer. Her books include *Through Parisian Eyes: Reflections on Contemporary French Arts and Culture* (1986), and *The Art of Love: Love Poems and Paintings* (1993). Her series *Luminous Bodies* derives its inspiration from Blake's work.

LMH is fortunate to own a collection of twentieth-century and contemporary art, with several works by outstanding women artists. The College regards this collection not as something static, but rather as a basis for continuing exploration of artistic creation in our society. Showing new work is vitally important. We were particularly pleased to show Melinda's work, because she is herself a former student of LMH, and this exhibition represented in a very direct way the College's ongoing commitment to the visual arts. We were most grateful that at the private view, Melinda generously donated two paintings from the Luminous Bodies series to the College to take their place in this collection. *Obituary* [Cover Painting, Pl. 90, Vol. 2, No. 3] and *You Find Infinity* [Cover Painting, Pl. 22, Vol. 2, No. 2] are powerfully evocative and complementary images. We are delighted that they continue and extend LMH's treasured living record of artistic creation. The very contemporaneity of the art is important for us, especially in this Jerwood Gallery series, which celebrates art and artists now, today.

But all artists work also in relation to the art of the past. The contemporary is always located in a response to what has gone before, as described by Peter Trippi in this volume. Because Melinda has been greatly influenced by William Blake, it is particularly appropriate that Blake scholar Robin Hamlyn should explore that influence with such subtlety and insight. His words are an excellent introduction to Melinda's luminous paintings [Vol. 2, No.3].

Dr. Frances Lannon
Principal of Lady Margaret Hall
Lady Margaret Hall
Oxford University
November 2004

Dr. Frances Lannon relaxing with Melinda Camber Porter before the Exhibition
November 2004
Lady Margaret Hall
Oxford University, United Kingdom
Photo: Joseph R Flicek

MELINDA CAMBER PORTER:
A NEW COSMOLOGY IN MODERN ART

While closely studying an artist's oeuvre, it is often helpful to step back and look at it afresh, through the eyes of someone who has never seen it before. Recently I showed Melinda Camber Porter's large, bright oils and small, cooler works on paper to a perceptive friend, who concluded, "They look of our time, but their spirit is timeless." Exactly, but why and how?

In our era of slickly produced images, teeming with messages rather than feelings, Camber Porter's pictures strike a distinctive balance between the achingly personal and the aesthetically beautiful. This equilibrium has developed, at least in part, through her discerning openness to a range of historical "mentors," William Blake being the figure she has admired most passionately (in fact, since she was six years old).[1] Unlike many artists working today, Camber Porter recognizes that exploring these interconnections neither limits her creativity nor renders her work derivative. Indeed, one lifetime was clearly not time enough for Blake to explore every avenue, so why wouldn't his strategies intrigue and engage subsequent generations, albeit in ways adapted to their own situations?

In her oils, Camber Porter is exploring terrain most recently combed by Marc Chagall: we find with both artists an expressive use of line and color masses to create compelling compositions that are seemingly weightless and freed from the quotidian demands of realism and perspective—swirling, dream-like visions of erotic and spiritual rapture. As *The Times* of London's cultural correspondent in Paris, Camber Porter exercised her eye everywhere in the city and surely encountered Chagall's work often, though she has wisely avoided the decorative excesses of his late career.

Camber Porter's inscription of her own poetry—complete or fragmentary, legible or partially erased—further enhances her pictures' power and possibilities. Yet Blake scholar Robin Hamlyn is right to note that, for both

---

[1] Camber Porter spoke about her relationship with Blake during *Inspiration, Influence, or Intrusion? How Do Historical Masterworks Inform Artmaking Now?*, a panel discussion convened by *Artists Talk on Art* on 17 November 2006 at the School of Visual Arts, New York.

Blake and Camber Porter, "the image illuminates the words far more than the other way around."[2] This integration makes use of Camber Porter's professional experiences in writing, which she has been doing much longer than painting and drawing. Words have never failed her, yet pictures offer opportunities for self-expression that words alone cannot.

Since 1985, Camber Porter has produced 15 different series of work, which dealer Walter Wickiser perceives as an evolving map of "her own cosmology."[3] His phrase is apt, especially because "cosmology" is not something we think about much anymore, at least outside academe. The cosmology of Christendom once defined every Westerner: for better or for worse, people understood where they stood in the universe, and where they were headed. Perhaps the exemplar of this moment most pertinent to Camber Porter is Michelangelo, whose conflation of the spiritual and the material, the chaste and the sensual, horrified and aroused his contemporaries even as it communicated the artist's highly personal understanding of God, man, and their interrelationship.

The Enlightenment banished the Christian cosmology from mainstream

Cover from William Blake's *Songs of Innocence and of Experience*, 1789
Printed and published by William Blake in 1794

discourse; now many of us drift along, seeking our own certainties, sometimes aware of other cosmologies still revered by the Chinese, Native Americans, Australian aborigines, and other residents of Earth. Blake regretted the emptiness of Deist rationalism, and spent his life trying to represent the soul and body as interconnected. By freeing his images and words from the tyranny of realism, he could revisit some of the universal themes considered by his idol, Michelangelo—Creation, the Last

[2] *William Blake Illuminates the Works of Melinda Camber Porter*, a lecture by Robin Hamlyn reprinted in a catalogue documenting an exhibition of Camber Porter's *Luminous Bodies* series at Jerwood Gallery at Lady Margaret Hall, Oxford University, 2 November 2004, p. 4.

[3] Walter Wickiser's introduction to the exhibition catalogue *Melinda Camber Porter: The Arousal of Nature*, 5 February–2 March 2005, Walter Wickiser Gallery, New York

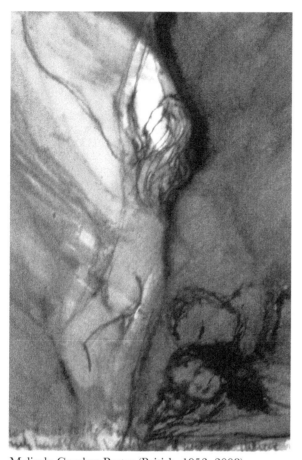

Melinda Camber Porter (British, 1953–2008)
The Dance of Love and Death Entwined. Then I Was Broken Lose From Death's Cold Feel, and Winged in Radiant Light (detail), 1995
Watercolor on paper
9 x 6 ½ inches
Luminious Bodies: First Circle, No. 15
Collection of Melinda Camber Porter Archive

Judgment, the Resurrection—while also exploring aspects of sensuality through such projects as *Songs of Innocence and of Experience*. Camber Porter's reverence for this volume is particularly keen, and we see in her *Art of Love* series how thoroughly she has personalized Blake's fascinations with the senses, and with the agonies and ecstasies of male-female relations.

Blake loomed large in the imagination of 19th-century British artists, especially the Pre-Raphaelite Dante Gabriel Rossetti and his fellow medievalist Edward Burne-Jones. Ostensibly focused upon his namesake, Dante, Rossetti actually emulated Blake through his deployment of pictures and poems—often together—to communicate his Romantic interlinkage of carnal passion and chaste spiritual love. It was only in one unfinished oil (*Dantis Amor*, 1860, Tate Britain) that Rossetti found the courage to abandon his realistic technique; with its flattened figure of Love standing between a sunburst of Christ and a crescent-moon of Beatrice, this image points emphatically toward the second generation of Pre-Raphaelitism being developed at just that moment by Burne-Jones.

Burne-Jones's proto-symbolist images surrounded Camber Porter as she grew up in England: his stained glass designs for Morris & Co. are found in churches nationwide, including Oxford, where Camber Porter was a student, and his paintings attained a psychedelic fashion ability among her generation. As we study Camber Porter's work, we see that—in contrast to her wholesale absorption of Blake—she looks to Burne-Jones not for his ascetic figures or muted colors, but for his ability to design a composition that sweeps viewers into his realm of dangerous passion (*Phyllis and Demophoön*) and eroticized lethargy (*King Cophetua and the Beggar Maid*). Having abandoned his divinity studies at Oxford for the cause of art, Burne-Jones spent the rest of his life creating his own cosmology, openly inspired by poets past and present, many of whom he knew personally. The largest of his pictures read as veritable altarpieces painted in homage to his feminine ideal, and one cannot help but ponder this fact while admiring Camber Porter's *Triptych* series.

That body of work led directly to her partnering with Elizabeth Swados on the rock opera, *Journey to Benares*. Even more than with Blake, music features in the capacity of Burne-Jones's complex designs to evoke all the senses: his positioning of figures and props provides a rhythm across the surface, and musical instruments feature prominently in many compositions. Late in life, Burne-Jones fulfilled a longstanding dream by designing sets and costumes for Sir Henry Irving's 1894 production of *King Arthur*; one can safely argue that *Journey to Benares* constitutes Camber Porter's own effort at *gesamtkunstwerk* (total work of art).

Journey to Benares points to another crucial feature of Camber Porter's cosmology—her openness to the worldviews of non-Western cultures that she has experienced for herself. This is not so unusual within her globetrotting generation, of course, but it also reflects the artistic influence of Paul Gauguin, whose own travel-inspired cosmology suited our century more than his. Shifting his attention from the "primitive" traditions of rural Brittany to those of Tahiti, Gauguin found in their stories what he needed to understand sex, nature, and life. Not surprisingly, Camber Porter finds particular pleasure in Gauguin's notebooks, which erase the boundaries between image and word. Through her *Badlands* series, and her novel of the same title, Camber Porter addresses her twin appreciation of Native spirituality and the rugged natural elements of South Dakota's Pine Ridge reservation. Because she lives in a more egalitarian era, however, we detect none of Gauguin's patronizing tone here. Such even-handedness is sustained in her *Luminous Bodies* series, here in two volumes of more than 100 works, which began when the loss of a loved one drove Camber Porter to explore traditions of mourning pursued in cultures around the world.

Without Gauguin's trailblazing, of course, Pierre Bonnard would not have been free to return again and again to hallucinatory images of his wife at home and in the garden. At once erotic and romantic, these scenes have clearly inspired Camber Porter with their brilliant palette and flickering light, but also with their disarming spatial ambiguity.

Melinda Camber Porter may visit museums often, read art books and reviews voraciously, and consult experts regularly, but a walk through her studio confirms that she has a voice of her own, and that her over 25 art series share a continuity of vision. This year, as the field reassesses and historicizes the impact of "feminist" artmaking after 1970, it is intriguing to observe that none of Camber Porter's most significant role models were female. This does not mean that she disdains Mary Cassatt or Georgia O'Keeffe, nor that other women have never experienced what Camber Porter feels yet it does suggest that in our relatively liberated times a woman artist can address such personally charged issues so boldly, without worrying about "propriety."

In an art market crowded with hollow protestations of "self-identity," Melinda Camber Porter's works offer us a new cosmology and a vision of our times. They are all the more valuable for having been informed by insights Camber Porter has gleaned from the past.

Peter Trippi
Editor, Fine Art Connoisseur
New York, 2010

INTRODUCTION
BY MELINDA CAMBER PORTER

*L*uminous Bodies is a work of mourning and an exploration of the spiritual and cultural forces that continuously vie to originate and then heal the rift between the body and the soul.

Inspired by many religious traditions of mourning, from *The Tibetan Book of the Dead* to Native American mourning rituals, the series of drawings is, in actuality, a spiritual journey begun by the artist a few days after the death of a loved one. The journey is narrated in drawings and in epigrammatic prose poetry inscribed within the images. There is a strong "documentary" aspect to the work, which attempts to record faithfully the actual process of loss and resurrection of the lover. Memory is revealed to be so much more than mere remembrance. For as the artist, recollects the love affair, she recreates the lover. At one juncture the artist writes that "those that one loves in one's heart and soul / will always accompany one." Memory becomes the sense that gives us access to the existence of a spiritual reality and leads us to the place where the spirit lives, even when

the body has disappeared. Though grief propels the imagery forward, the sense of retrieving love and creating love beyond the grip of death infuses these drawings with a luminous joy. Some have compared the journey taken in *Luminous Bodies* to Christ's journey through the Stations of the Cross.

But whereas in much Judeo-Christian philosophy the body is seen as the weak vehicle, the Achilles heel that catapults man into sin, *Luminous Bodies* proposes a world view that gives back to the body its sacrosanct nature. Human ecstasy, when body and soul unite, is the experience which is perpetually recollected and meditated upon and that serves as the pivotal visual perspective. From this vantage point a philosophical viewpoint of existence is etched, both visually and in poetry. Thus, for example, in my poem:

> *The Spirit and Body are one.*
> *The physical world contains*
> *the juice of the fruit.*
> *When the skin of the fruit is peeled off,*
> *we drink in each other's souls.*

In a further nudity.
Always striving for a further
unpeeling of the mask.
Sometimes I think I might
have saved you from death.

Much as Blake's visual and poetic works contained a complex cosmology, so does the *Luminous Bodies Series*. The series posits a world where, paradoxically, clear-sightedness seems only to arise from intense passion.

As the journey taken in *Luminous Bodies Series* progresses, the notion of the sacred springs from the image of the human body and as such shares with much Indian art (and particularly tantric art) the belief that the erotic can be the pathway to enlightenment. Just as man was returned to center stage in the Renaissance and a new appreciation of humanity was celebrated in the fine arts, similarly, in *Luminous Bodies* the human body is seen as a microcosm for the cosmos, and human narrative and emotion take center stage.

The *Luminous Bodies* series comprises ninety-one works on paper, varying from 9 ½ x 11 inches to 6 ½ by 9 inches, which were selected from hundreds of my works on paper. The ninety one water colors are arranged in six circles of mourning and celebration with three circles in each of two volumes. The circles of mourning and celebration are in a way the spiritual nature of both life and death which we all in our own ways experience.

On William Blake's Title page of *Songs of Innocence and of Experience* [Kings College of Cambridge] the cover text says, "showing the two contrary states of the human soul."

The first of copy of *Songs of Innocence* was given to me when I was six years old. It was popular and somehow was given to children with its success based on a misunderstanding. As there was much more to it as Baudelaire describes it: "L'étude du beau est un duel où l'artiste crie de frayeur avant d'être vaincu." [The study of beauty is a duel in which the artist cries out in terror before being defeated.] In other words 'There are an array of emotions—'

Blake communicated in colors, movement and feeling rather than pure intellect. Blake also showed me the beauty of communicating in poetry and painting, text and image as the text and image that are shown in Blake's *The Garden of Love* from *Songs of Innocence and of Experience* [Kings College of Cambridge].

I paint in both oils on canvas and small works on paper and always in series. I'm excited by the relationship between the words that pass through my mind when I am painting the actual images.

In my painting, *Myself Inscribed in Nature* [*Barcelona Point Series*], with text inscribed at top of canvas: "I want your hands inside me your lips inside me" and at bottom of canvas: "the liquid of desire [lines erased] between our souls."

when I do this, because it tells me the painting is taking off. So I want the words to help me tell the story.

The *Luminous Bodies Series* consists of ninety small works on paper that describe

Melinda Camber Porter's brushes and tools from her studio
Collection of the Melinda Camber Porter Archive
Photo: Joseph R. Flicek

In my painting, *Before the damage* [*Triptych Series*] you will see when I am painting, I'll erase words on the painting, when I feel that they have been better described by an image I'm painting or a color I am using. I often get a sense of deep relief

a spiritual journey I took when a man I was in love with many years ago suddenly died.

There are poems inscribed in a Blakean way in the images of *Luminous Bodies*. The poem doesn't really illustrate the words. The words are born by arising from the moment of doing the painting.

Let me say something about the words in *Luminous Bodies*. Sometimes I don't need too many words with an image and other times I may have a complete poem as in *La Semence* [Pl. 54, Vol. 2, No. 3]. Text is pen and ink on watercolor with erased upper inscription and poem on right.

> "les pierres de Paris regorgent
>   la sémence
> des siècles des amants...
>   leurs doigts
> posés sur mes yeux pour que
>   mon âme
> seule, s'est montrée; mes seins
> palpitent avec l'esprit d'image;
> et puis, je me suis
>   échappée, je
> me suis fondue en larmes; les
> années sont passées; j'étais
>   en exil
> mais les souffles que je respire
> sont remplis de toi, ouverte,
>   encore
> une fois, avec toi"

But I did want to highlight that the redness in *La Semence* is warmth and it envelopes the whole world when you are in love.

In my painting, *The World is Warm Again* [Pl. 7] the text sometimes describes what's actually happening, it's like a diary insert, but often it is of a dream or a visitation from the spirit of the deceased person or sometimes it's just a memory.

In my painting, *But You Always Returned Claiming Me Completely*, [Pl. 58, Vol. 2, No. 3] which is a watercolor and pen and ink drawing with inscription, "I tried to teach myself to love elsewhere; spent years trying, but you always returned, claiming me, completely. January 1996."

Blake gave me a great deal of familiarity with spiritual painting or rendering visible spiritual realities. People thought Blake saw things, and was crazy. But he wasn't. He knew the difference between fantasy and imagination. He believed in the power of imagination. He wasn't interested at all in pure fantasy as let's say Dalí or Redon were.

The soul hovering over the body reluctantly parting with life is from Blair's *The Grave* [British Museum]. Blake was commissioned by the engraver and would-be publisher Robert H. Cromek to prepare forty drawings illustrating Robert Blair's *The Grave*, a popular "Graveyard" school poem first published in 1743 and used only twenty of Blake's drawings.

In the *Luminous Bodies Series*, because my past relationship was rather erotically charged and because the person's body had passed on, I also thought about something I've always been obsessed with which is the spiritual nature of sex. This is an idea that Blake championed. He also championed women's right to enjoy sex and to be sexual beings, which was pretty revolutionary for his time.

I suppose I had this sad moment when I remembered the person now dead. This is what sparked off the *Luminous Bodies Series*. 'The Body and Soul are One' and the realization that it was a totally joyful experience.

Being a woman and giving birth to two children and breast feeding both of them also made me very aware of the amazing genius of the human body and its divine nature.

In my painting, *Fertility of Buried Souls* [Pl. 80, Vol. 2, No. 2] which is a watercolor with an inscription, "Years after our souls met, we became friends. We dropped our passion on the floor, we forgave each other. We began a new journey, venturing near each other's souls through kindness, affection, mutual respect. And then, you died, as if I had only been given you yet again in order to say goodbye. Obituary. February 1996."

Blake and Catherine, his wife, never had children, but he obviously had a deep respect for women. He treated his wife Catherine as an equal and although she wasn't educated he encouraged her to get involved with his intellectual life and she colored many of his engravings and collaborated with him successfully.

I feel when I look at Blake, this sense of human companionship, which Blake offers the spectator. Many artists fill one with awe, like Dürer or Piero della Francesca or Cézanne. But Blake never strives for complete perfection. He'll go for the energetic sweep of the pen rather than getting the muscles in the right position.

One of Blake's works that has inspired me over and over again is called the *Whirlwind of Lovers*. There are several versions of it: I have seen the engraving in black and white in the library at the British Museum. I remember light falling, the mystical moment, and I could feel him in the room. The one you see is actually more stunning I suppose. It's in Manchester. And it sums up for me the grandeur of Blake's genius.

In the painting, you see this celestial light and the two lovers, who are Francesca da Rimini and Paulo [Malatesta]. They were killed by Paulo's brother, because they were adulterous lovers, as Francesca was having an affair with her husband's brother. Dante and Virgil show shame, but not Blake who corrects Dante's punitive vision in The Circle of the Lustful from *The Divine Comedy* [Birmingham Museum and Art Gallery]. Blake actually puts the lovers in a celestial light and not in shame.

I've always been fascinated by Blake's 'Luminosity' quite literary because it's a kind of light that burns away fear and hypocrisy and repression and it allows you to see.

Melinda Camber Porter's brushes and tools from her studio
Collection of the Melinda Camber Porter Archive
Photo: Joseph R. Flicek

In my own work, I love the watercolor paper because if you use it as a source of light—it radiates. In my painting from *Luminous Bodies* I wanted the white and empty spaces of the paper to be as vibrant as the lines I draw.

In my oils I've tried to use the white canvas as I do the watercolor paper. It's harder to do because oil paint is thick and somehow seems to be more vibrant and more present than white spaces. Sometimes people ask me, "is the painting finished" and I say it is! An example is my oil painting, "Is this what you asked of me?" from the *Triptych Series*. My idea here was to use a sacred form something you would associate with a church, and insert erotic subject matter. The woman on the right is fully painted, but the one in the middle who is flying and is airborne isn't fully painted. You'd need to see the painting to make up your own mind as to whether I succeeded in making the white space luminous, reproductions never do justice to empty space on a canvas.

In my oil painting, *Horse Grazing by Lovers* from the *Horses of Chauvet Series*, people often think it's a charcoal mixed with pen and ink. This pleases me, because it means I've used the empty white space as fully a pigment part of the oil painting.

The oil painting, *Stories in Waiting* from the *Triptych Series*, is a painting that I had

on my easel not because I hadn't finished it, but because I wanted to reflect on it. When the art historian, Jason Rosenberg, visited my studio, he was fascinated by the painting and it sparked off a discussion on my obsession with luminosity. *Stories in Waiting* has large amounts of empty canvas, which is crucial to the painting. It was tempting to overpaint and fill in the empty spaces. But I knew I had finished the painting, and I didn't give into the temptation to paint in the bodies which were represented by outlines only. I knew I didn't want to fill them in.

In my painting of Shiva and Parvati from the *Triptych* series, the rage of passion is so vibrant that it was an interesting challenge to make the whiteness of the bodies transcendent. I suppose in this case the lovers are just part of the flow of energy in the world. Everything happens in waves. As it does in the ocean, they're in an ocean of fire and red hot desire. And their bodies are somehow fed from having a conventional defined shape as they could be tendrils curling round a tree or it could be the way they feel that's painted. Not the way an intruder would say they looked.

So, like Blake I want to free the body from its representative realistic shape and let it be anything at all.

In my painting, *Shiva and Parvati in the*

Forest from the *Triptych Series* I used the mythology of Shiva and Parvati to help me do this. Shiva and Parvati as many Indian gods have over a 1000 different manifestations, as when they make love, their dance of life begins. Their unity is celebrated all over Benares in the form of Linga, which show the male and female abstractly as a unity.

This painting and other paintings in the *Triptych Series* inspired the creation of a rock opera called, *Journey to Benares*. The *Triptych* paintings themselves inspired Elizabeth Swados to write a musical score and *Journey to Benares* was born. The *Triptych* paintings were then used as the set design at the Asia Society and Museum for the stage performance. I am always excited that art has a life of its own over and above the actions and intentions of the artist. The paintings inspired Elizabeth Swados to write music. And this happened all happened out of the blue when Blake's works crept into my mind and obsessed me from the age of six. When I do a painting I don't consciously copy Blake, but works of his suddenly help me to complete a particular brushstroke or a line of a poem of his will soothe me when I'm feeling particularly tortured about navigating my way through a canvas. Most of it isn't conscious. But in the case of Blake, I have a lot to thank him for. It would have been a much lonelier path for me, doing the kind of work I do, without him.

Melinda Camber Porter
From *Artists Talk on Art*
The School of Visual Arts
New York
November 2, 2006

LUMINOUS BODIES

CIRCLES OF CELEBRATION

First Circle

of

Celebration and Mourning

You resurrected hope and drowned it, in one motion. Dec 23 95 Melinda

You Resurrected Hope

1995
Watercolor on paper
9 x 6 ½ inches

Luminious Bodies: First Circle
No.1

Inscription: "*You resurrected hope and drowned it, in one motion. Dec 23 95 Melinda*"

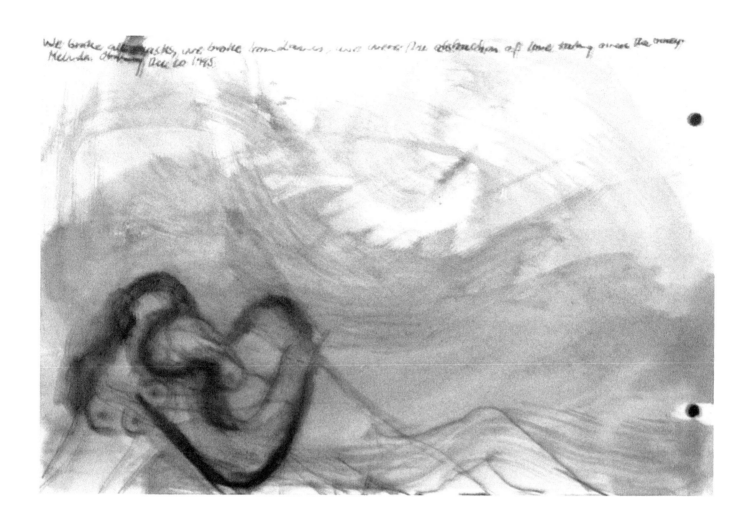

We Broke All Masks

1995
Watercolor on paper
9 x 6 ½ inches

Luminious Bodies: First Circle
No. 2

Inscription: *"We broke all masks, we broke boundaries, we were the abstraction of love taking over the body. Melinda Obituary Dec 10 1995"*

Returned to Pure Dream

1995
Watercolor on paper
9 x 6 ½ inches

Luminious Bodies: First Circle
No. 3

Inscription: *"I slept like a child on your crossed legs, returned to pure dream and to longing. Obituary Melinda Dec 20 95"*

Pont du Carrousel

1995
Watercolor on paper
9 x 6 ½ inches

Luminious Bodies: First Circle
No. 4

Inscription, upper: *"The river of death brings me memories of all those I ever loved. Dec 20 95 Melinda"*

Inscription, lower: *"Pont du Carousel"*

Vertigo

1995
Watercolor on paper
9 x 6 ½ inches

Luminious Bodies: First Circle
No. 5

Inscription: *"Vertigo Obituary Dec 22 95 Melinda"*

I Can Touch Us Now As If You Are Alive

1995
Watercolor on paper
9 x 6 ½ inches

Luminious Bodies: First Circle
No. 6

Inscription, upper, almost erased: *"My belief, over and above everything, I tried in love, was that passion was destructive. 20 years after I met you I want passion to arise and fire my life again* [erased] *I want to hold the life force in my hand."*

Inscription, lower: *"Melinda Obituary, Dec 22 1995"*

The World Is Warm Again

1995
Watercolor on paper
9 x 6 ½ inches

Luminious Bodies: First Circle
No. 7

Inscription: *"The world is warm again. Obituary Dec 22 95 Melinda"*

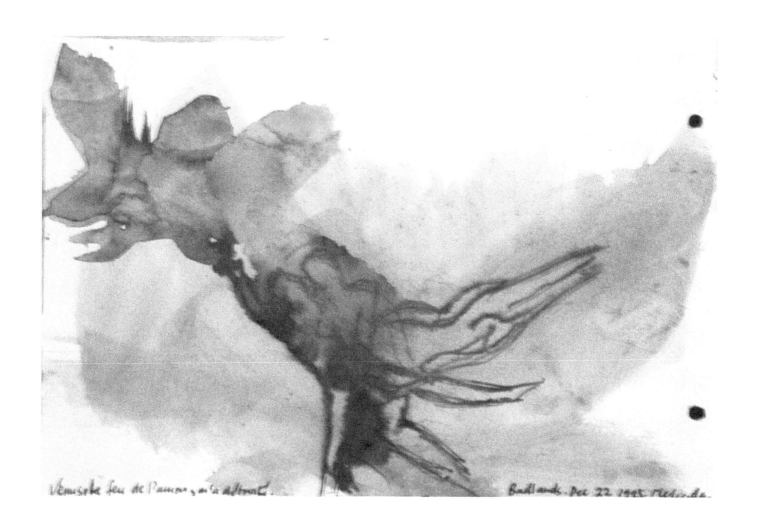

Vénus, Le Feu de L'amour

1995
Watercolor on paper
9 x 6 ½ inches

**Luminious Bodies: First Circle
No. 8**

Inscription: *"Vénus, le feu de l'amour, m'a détruite."*

Inscription, lower right: *"Badlands Dec 22 1995 Melinda"*

I'm Unable to Move Out of Grief

1995
Watercolor on paper
9 x 6 ½ inches

Luminious Bodies: First Circle
No. 9

Inscription: *"I'm unable to move out of grief. Melinda Dec 24 1995"*

The Flesh Broke Open

1995
Watercolor on paper
9 x 6 ½ inches

Luminious Bodies: First Circle
No. 10

Inscription: *"The flesh broke open—where you entered my soul and never closed up again. Obituary Dec 27 1995 Melinda"*

Remembrance of the Resurrection

1995
Watercolor on paper
9 x 6 ½ inches

Luminious Bodies: Which Circle
No. 11

Inscription: *"The Remembrance of the Resurrection Dec 24 1995"*

Then Nature and the Earth Became Kinder

1995
Watercolor on paper
9 x 6 ½ inches

Luminious Bodies: First Circle
No. 12

Inscription: *"Then Nature and the earth became kinder for I gave her my tears of grief. Melinda 95 Dec 25"*

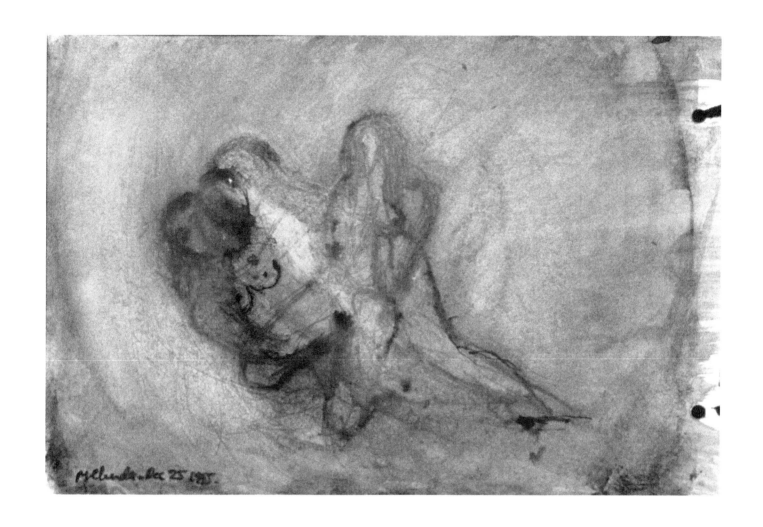

Myselves in You

1995
Watercolor on paper
9 x 6 ½ inches

**Luminious Bodies: First Circle
No. 13**

Inscription: *"Melinda Dec 25 1995"*

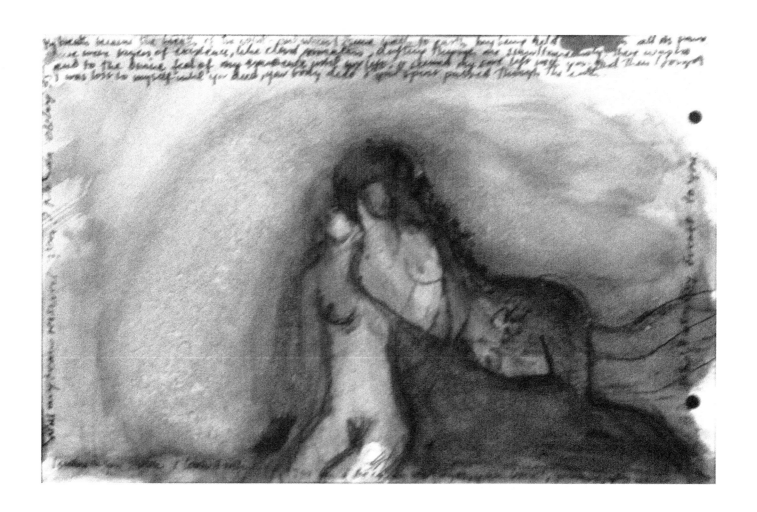

My Breath Became the Breath of the Spirit

1995
Watercolor on paper
9 x 6 ½ inches

Luminious Bodies: First Circle
No. 14

Inscription, upper: *"My breath became the breath of the spirit—and when I came back to Earth my being held* [erased]*...in all its power. There were layers of existence, like cloud formations, drifting through me simultaneously. There was no end to the divine feel of my existence until you left. It seemed my soul left with you. And then I forgot I was lost to myself until you died, your body died and your spirit pulsed through the earth."*

Inscription, bottom: *"I swam in your vision* [erased] *I became your eyes, your breast* [erased]*."*

Inspection, left: *"Will my tears resurrect you? Melinda Obituary 95"*

Inspection, right: *"I held my breast to you"*

The Dance of Love and Death Entwined. Then I Was Broken Lose From Death's Cold Feel, and Winged in Radiant Light

1995
Watercolor on paper
9 x 6 ½ inches

**Luminious Bodies: First Circle
No. 15**

Inscription: *"Somehow in my Dance to life* [erased] *of abandon, your image will slip through my hands and I will see a new face where you lay inside me. Melinda 1995"*

Then He Left Me and the Night Was Calm

1995
Watercolor on paper
9 x 6 ½ inches

Luminious Bodies: First Circle
No. 16

Inscription: *"Somehow in my dance to life I will retrieve you* [erased] *as a beginning, not as an end to ecstasy. With my love for you still rising in me, I let your soul leave me for good, as the man who owns my body and soul. Dec.* [erased] *Then he left me, and the night was calm and I was not alone."*

If I can move and paint and live on this line where the soul's ecstasy floods the body of life and death, if I can move where you took me, out into the night sky, into pure breath of infinity, if I can draw these lines given to me— then the curves must always show a dance to life, even though your death is still my lover, even though you still lead me, even though I still mourn you and so my journey takes me into the loss of you and is not fully in unison with the life force of the living.

Give me strength to go on this journey until I forget our love in a new form, not only on the page but in my flesh, in my breath, again, and again.

Give Me the Strength to Go on This Journey

1995
Watercolor on paper
9 x 6 ½ inches

Luminious Bodies: First Circle
No. 17

Inscription, upper: *"If I can move and paint and live on this line where the soul's ecstasy floods the body of life and death, if I can move where you took me, out into the night sky, into pure breath of infinity, if I can draw these lines given to me— then the curves must always show a dance to life, even though your death is still my lover, even though you still lead me, even though I still mourn you and so my journey takes me into the loss of you and is not fully in unison with the life force of the living.*

Give me the strength to go on this journey until I forget our love in a new form, not only on the page but in my flesh, in my breath, again, and again."

Inscript, lower: *"Melinda, Dec 1995"*

Second Circle
of
Celebration and Mourning

This story of two worlds—the world of vision and spirit—and the world of sorrow and confusion—took place in our meeting in the flesh. It was in our bodies that the truth lay and our emotions were sacred. We are the flow of the seasons. We are the flowering of hope in spring. We are the cold featureless landscape in winter, iced over with death. You are flame and ice. Life and Death. You are my capacity to love. I follow your soul's progress.

Melinda 1995 Dec 4th

This Story of Two Worlds

1995
Pen and ink, watercolor on paper
11 x 9 ½ inches

Luminious Bodies: Second Circle
No. 18

Inscription, upper: *"This story of two worlds—the world of vision and spirit—and the world of sorrow and confusion—took place in our meeting in the flesh. It was in our bodies that the truth lay and our emotions were sacred. We are the flow of the seasons. We are the flowering of hope in spring. We are the cold featureless landscape in winter, iced over with death. You are flame and ice. Life and Death. You are my capacity to love. I follow your soul's progress."*

Inscription, lower: *"Melinda 1995 Dec 4th"*

You will leave me in the salt of my tears. Leave room for me to find you again, what you gave to me, in another. If I want the exact feel of your voice, your hands on me, then half of me will live in memory, half in the grave. Let me abstract you from your corpse and embody you in a new form. Dec 5 95.

For the river of life to flow through us.   *Melinda.*

You Will Leave Me in the Salt of My Tears

1995
Pen and ink on paper
11 x 9 ½ inches

Luminious Bodies: Second Circle
No. 19

Inscription, upper: *"You will leave me in the salt of my tears. Leave room for me to find you again, what you gave to me, in another. If I want the exact feel of your voice, your hands on me, then half of me will live in memory, half in the grave. Let me abstract you from your corpse and embody you in a new form. Dec 5 1995."*

Inscription, lower: *"For the river of life to flow through us. Melinda"*

All the Ecstasy I Never Felt Before, I Felt in You

1995
Pen and ink on paper
11 x 9 ½ inches

Luminious Bodies: Second Circle
No. 20

Inscription: *"All the mourning I never did, I do in you. All the ecstasy I never felt before, I felt in you. Dec 6th 95"*

All these years went by, two decades, and always, I left a part of my soul in us. Now you are dead, only now, do I know you took me down to the grave with you, as you had taken me through you life. I will not be afraid of this knowledge, because I will love again.

Melinda Dec 6

I Will Not Be Afraid

1995
Pen and ink on paper
11 x 9 ½ inches

Luminious Bodies: Second Circle
No. 21

Inscription, upper: *"All these years went by, two decades, and always, I left a part of my soul in us. Now you are dead, only now, do I know you took me down to the grave with you, as you had taken me through your life. I will not be afraid of this knowledge, because I will love again."*

Inscription, lower: *"Melinda Dec 6th"*

You find infinity with one or two people in your life. He said. sometimes you spread it over lots of encounters. It depends how much of it you can take. I will open the doors and take it now you are gone. Dec 6th 95. The sky is bruised with overflowing light

You Find Infinity

1995
Pen and ink, watercolor on paper
11 x 9 ½ inches

Luminious Bodies: Second Circle
No. 22

Inscription: *"'You find infinity with one or two people in your life,' he said. 'Sometimes you spread it over lots of encounters. It depends on how much of it you can take.' I will open the doors and take it now you are gone. Dec 6th 1995. The sky is bruised with overflowing light."*

My self regained, my self was lost in you. Joy floated down the river of death. I saw my face in yours. Our child in me, drifting beyond my grasp. Blood fell from you and merged with the stream of consciousness. You opened out, petals, star shaped, sky and earth blossoming from your death.

Melinda Dec7 1995.

I Saw My Face in Yours

1995
Sepia pen and ink on paper
11 x 9 ½ inches

Luminious Bodies: Second Circle
No. 23

Inscription, upper: *"My self regained, my self was lost in you. Joy floated down the river of death. I saw my face in yours. Our child in me, drifting beyond my grasp."*

Inscription, lower: *"Melinda Dec 7 1995"*

Drown Me in You

1995
Sepia pen and ink on paper
11 x 9 ½ inches

Luminious Bodies: Second Circle
No. 24

Inscription, upper: *"Bathe me in your memory, so I can resurrect you. I miss you. Take me down with you into your spirit so I can breathe again. Take me on your journey, drown me in you, so I can become part of the tree of life."*

Inscription, lower: *"Melinda Dec 7 95."*

rue de Ponthieu - Melinda Dec 8.95.

Rue de Ponthieu

1995
Pen and ink on paper
11 x 9 ½ inches

Luminious Bodies: Second Circle
No. 25

Inscription: *"Rue de Ponthieu Melinda Dec 8 95"*

L'Inde Fantome

1995
Pen and ink on paper
11 x 9 ½ inches

Luminious Bodies: Second Circle
No. 26

Inscription: *"L'Inde Fantome. Central Park West. Melinda Dec 8 1995"*

Staking Out Territory

1995
Sepia pen and ink on paper
11 x 9 ½ inches

Luminious Bodies: Second Circle
No. 27

Inscription: "*Staking out territory in the world of desire. Breaking open memory, passing out beyond death. Dec 8 1995. Melinda*"

Your Breath on Me

1995
Sepia pen and ink on paper
11 x 9 ½ inches

Luminious Bodies: Second Circle
No. 28

Inscription: *"You handed me back to the living when you died. I feel your breath on me. Dec 8 1995. Melinda"*

Betrayal

1995
Pen and ink on paper
11 x 9 ½ inches

Luminious Bodies: Second Circle
No. 29

Inscription: *"Betrayal. New York City. Dec 9 1995. I found you in her arms, all over again, even in your death."*

Through Bitterness

1995
Sepia pen and ink on paper
11 x 9 ½ inches

Luminious Bodies: Second Circle
No. 30

Inscription: *"Losing you again, through bitterness. Melinda 1995. Dec 4. Obituary. I will not. These works will be for you, too, in memory of you."*

On the rim of the earth, I hold you with all my strength outside of loss. Does that not speak of love between us? Dec 1995. 9
Obituary. Melinda.

I Hold You with All My Stength Outside of Loss

1995
Sepia pen and ink on paper
11 x 9 ½ inches

**Luminious Bodies: Second Circle
No. 31**

Inscription: *"On the rim of the earth, I hold you with all my strength outside of loss. Does that not speak of love between us? Dec 1995. 9.*
Obituary. Melinda"

Obituary Dec 95 Melinda.

Lovers Arising as the Crescent Moon

1995
Pen and ink on paper
11 x 9 ½ inches

Luminious Bodies: Second Circle
No. 32

Inscription: *"Obituary Dec 1995 Melinda"*

Obituary Dec 10 1995. Melinda

Bathed in Your Image

1995
Pen and ink, watercolor on paper
11 x 9 ½ inches

**Luminious Bodies: Second Circle
No. 33**

Inscription: *"Obituary Dec 10 1995 Melinda"*

For Joe. The Resolution. Dec 10 1995. Melinda

Resolution

1995
Pen and ink, watercolor on paper
11 x 9 ½ inches

Luminious Bodies: Which Circle
No. 34

Inscription: *"For Joe. The Resolution. Dec 10 1995. Melinda"*

THIRD CIRCLE

OF

CELEBRATION AND MOURNING

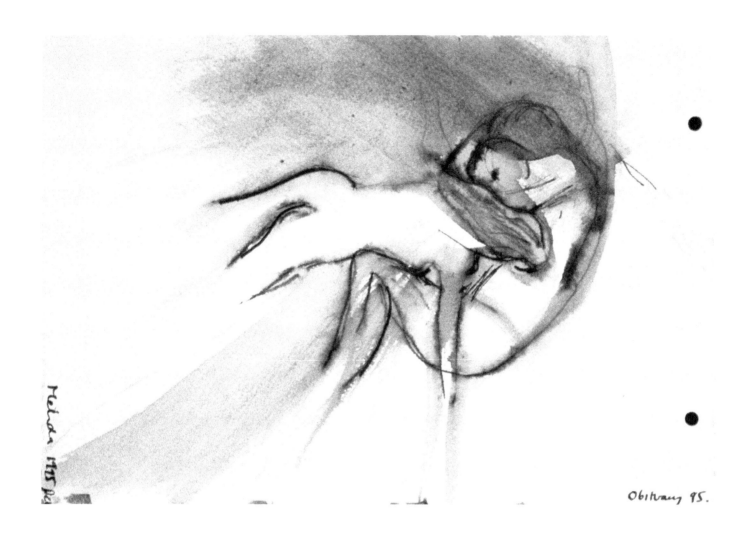

Merging Within Your Death

1995
Pen and ink on paper
9 x 6 ½ inches

**Luminious Bodies: Third Circle
No. 35**

Inscription, lower left: *"Melinda 1995 Dec"*

Inscription, lower right: *"Obituary 95."*

Listen to the Dead

1995
Pen and ink, watercolor on paper
9 x 6 ½ inches

Luminious Bodies: Third Circle
No. 36

Inscription: *"To understand how the soul achieves immortality requires complete receptivity to each sensation—trusting each thought that arises when one loses the loved one. Each intuition will defy logic. So listen even when in tears. We must listen to the dead, the body dissolving, tears [word illegible] over our ability to think, so the thoughts seem like madness. Still, we must listen to the dissolving other and learn. I hold you now before you fall back to the earth. Dec 95. Melinda."*

In you was the journey of the true artist. You were like Christ, imbibing our conflicts to embody them so we could feel again. You did this for me

You are the bridge from the living to the dead. We are the bridge above your rising body. Already the grass rises over your tomb. I will not forget you.

Wave upon Wave of My Tears

1995
Pen and ink, watercolor on paper
9 x 6 ½ inches

Luminious Bodies: Third Circle
No. 37

Inscription, upper: *"In you was the journey of the true artist. You were like Christ, imbibing our conflicts to embody them so we could feel again. You did this for me"*

Inscription, lower: *"You are the bridge from the living to the dead. We are the bridge above your rising body. Already the grass rises over your tomb. I will not forget you."*

Le Pont de tes Cuisses. Mère, Amant, Rêve, Mon Rêve

1995
Pen and ink on paper
9 x 6 ½ inches

Luminious Bodies: Third Circle
No. 38

Inscription, upper: *"A few weeks after we met, I went to Cabourg, where Proust wrote A La recherche, to forget you. I went with a friend of yours. How could I forget you in his arms? We were writing together a screenplay. Cabourg was grey. The French provinces were always grey in my mind. How could I forget you in your friend's arms? No. I wanted you, not him. It was torment trying to bury you in the making love with your friend. Years later, I am going to Cape May, the Grand Hotel. Grand Hotel, Cabourg—years later. This time I am retrieving you. Perhaps for the first time. Retrieving in full, my love for you. All of my stray selves united for you, to be with you. Melinda. 1995"*

Inscription, lower: *"l'arc de mes seins*
traduit le pont neuf
le pont de tes cuisses
mère, amant, rêve, mon amant."

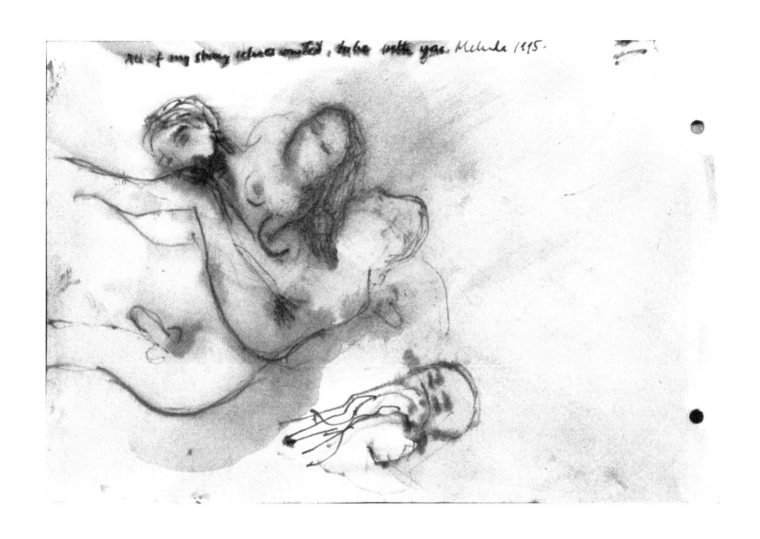

All of My Stray Selves United To Be with You

1995
Pen and ink on paper
9 x 6 ½ inches

Luminious Bodies: Third Circle
No. 39

Inscription: *"All of my stray selves united, to be with you. Melinda 1995."*

On the Boundaries of Flesh

1995
Pen and ink on paper
9 x 6 ½ inches

Luminious Bodies: Third Circle
No. 40

Inscription: *"All of my selves united to merge in you. Then the life force flowed through us and we still retained our definition on the boundaries of flesh. Melinda 1995."*

La Vierge et L'Amant

1995
Watercolor on paper
9 x 6 ½ inches

Luminious Bodies: Third Circle
No. 41

Inscription: *"Melinda Dec 95. La vierge et l'amant"*

Infinity of Existence

1995
Sepia pen and ink, watercolor on paper
9 x 6 ½ inches

Luminious Bodies: Third Circle
No. 42

Inscription: *"Alight with fire in my heart and soul, my mind dripping wet with desire, I open to you, in an infinity of existence. Dec 1995. The world of my soul verged close to my imagination. Then the wall between them broke when you died."*

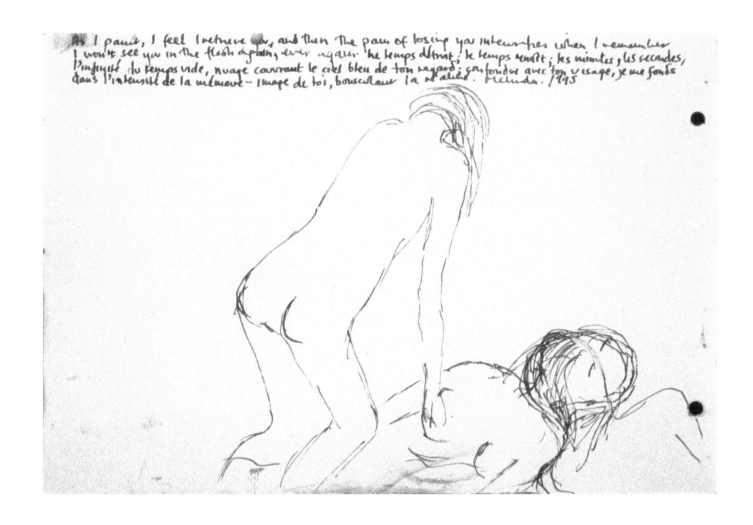

As I Paint I Retrieve You

1995
Sepia pen and ink on paper
9 x 6 ½ inches

Luminious Bodies: Third Circle
No. 43

Inscription: *"As I paint, I feel I retrieve you, and then the pain of losing you intensifies when I remember I won't see you in the flesh, ever again. Le temps détruit; le temps renaît; les minutes, les secondes, l'infinité du temps vide, nuage courant le ciel bleu de ton regard; confondue avec ton visage, je me fonds dans l'intensité de la mémoire—image de toi, bousculant la realitée. Melinda. 1995"*

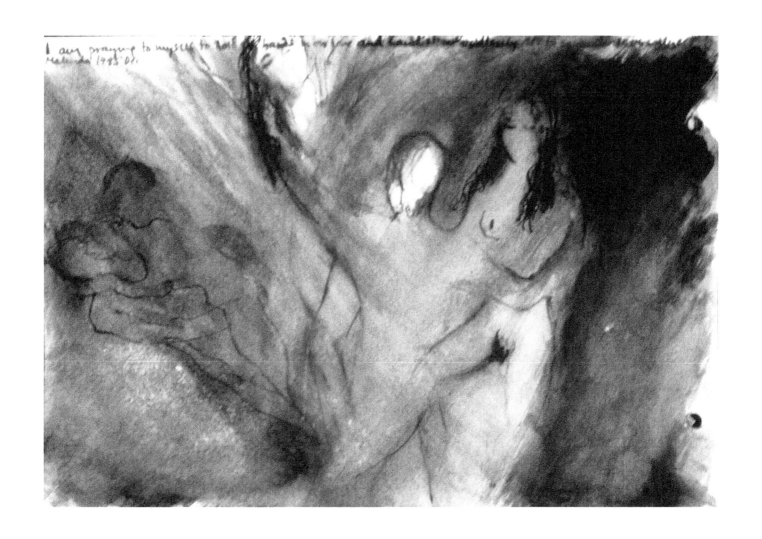

Prayer to Myself

1995
Watercolor on paper
9 x 6 ½ inches

**Luminious Bodies: Third Circle
No. 44**

Inscription: *"I am praying to myself to hold* [erased] *hands* [rest of inscription erased] *Melinda 1995 Dec."*

Poem. "Spirit Arising from Imagination"

1995
Pen and ink on paper
9 x 6 ½ inches

Luminious Bodies: Which Circle
No. 45

Inscription, upper: *"In between certainty and self-hatred, in between desire and shame, lies my understanding. Was it in your being that I found the way of thinking that would let me be free again? Each time I think of you I love you and lose your flesh. Will you become pure spirit? I imagine so. It was distilled in our meeting, what I desired from myself and another. A story that lived underground in me, so for years, I didn't even know that I felt anything for you; I prided myself on feeling nothing; So now, I want to make a memorial to you, to us, to what we got from each other, which is now mine."*

Inscription, center:
Join me together in one being
Spirit arising from imagination
—
Down in the breath of sleep
I had a dream of weeping
for my heart; you had dug
a place in your thighs where she
slept willingly. I wept
night long for myself;
in the morning I spoke in
my own voice; I felt my
breath warming me.
—
Join me together in one being
Spirit arising from imagination."

Inscription, bottom: *"Dec 1995"*

Melinda Camber Porter, 1983
Collection of the Melinda Camber Porter Archive
Photo: Joyce Baronio

MELINDA CAMBER PORTER
British, 1953–2008

Melinda Camber Porter was born in London and graduated from Oxford University with a First Class Honors degree in Modern Languages. She began her writing career in Paris as a cultural correspondent for *The Times* of London. French culture is the subject of her book *Through Parisian Eyes* (published by Oxford University Press), which the *Boston Globe* describes as "a particularly readable and brilliantly and uniquely compiled collection."

She interviewed many leading cultural figures in film and literature from Europe and America over her career. These included Nobel Prize winners Saul Bellow, Gunter Grass, Eugenio Montale, and Octavio Paz, writers including Joyce Carol Oates, Joan Didion, and Frances Sagan, and filmmakers Michael Apted, Martin Scorsese, and Wim Wenders, among many others. [Audio recordings are available for more than fifty of these cultural interviews.]

Her novel *Badlands*, a Book-of-the-Month Club selection, was set on South Dakota's Pine Ridge Indian Reservation and acclaimed by Louis Malle, who said: "better than a novel, it reads like a fierce poem, with a devastating effect on our self-esteem," and by *Publishers Weekly*, which called it, "a novel of startling, dreamlike lyricism."

A traveling art exhibition celebrating Camber Porter's paintings, curated by the late Leo Castelli, opened at the French Embassy in New York City in 1993. This exhibition, sponsored by the National Endowment for the Arts and the French Embassy, traveled to cities across the United States through 1997.

Peter Trippi, Editor of *Fine Art Connoisseur* magazine said: "In our era of slickly produced images, teeming with messages rather than feelings, Camber Porter's art strikes a distinctive balance between the achingly personal and the aesthetically beautiful. This equilibrium has developed, at least in part, through her discerning openness to a range of historical *mentors*, William Blake being the figure she has admired most passionately," and "not surprisingly Camber Porter finds particular pleasure in Gauguin's notebooks, which erase the boundaries between image and word."

A film documenting the creation of her paintings featured in the art exhibition *The Art of Love* showed regularly on Public Television stations nationally, and a collection of her poetry and paintings, also entitled *The Art of Love*, served as companion to the show.

Camber Porter's paintings have also served as the primary inspiration and as backdrops for several of her theatrical works. She created the backdrops, book, and lyrics for the musical *Night Angel*, with music by Carman Moore, which was originally performed at The Clark Theater, Lincoln Center, in New York City. She created the book, lyrics, and backdrops for the rock-opera-in-progress, *Journey to Benares*, with music, direction, and choreography by Elizabeth Swados, which was performed at the Asia Society and Museum in New York City in November 2003.

Robin Hamlyn, noted world expert on William Blake and senior curator of Tate Britain's Blake and Turner collections, delivered a lecture and wrote a book on Ms. Porter's watercolors entitled, *William Blake Illuminates the Works of Melinda Camber Porter*. Mr. Hamlyn writes about Ms. Porter, "I believe that all great art is, in its essence, defined by fearlessness. Both Melinda Camber Porter's and William Blake's works exemplify and illuminate the fearlessness that is part of the very essence of all great art."

Melinda Camber Porter leaves a prolific and creative legacy with thousands of paintings; over two hundred hours of audio and film interviews with global creative figures in the arts, film, and literature; and her tens of thousands of pages of writings: novels, plays, essays, journalism, and volumes of poetry. Her creative and spiritual works will be enjoyed for generations to come.

(www.MelindaCamberPorter.com)

PUBLIC ART EXHIBITIONS

2010

   Memorial, Buffalo Ridge, Gary, South Dakota

   Memorial, Clarke Theater, Lincoln Center, New York

   Retrospective, John Jermain Library, Sag Harbor, New York

2009

   Sag Harbor Tree Fund, Sag Harbor, New York

2008

   Memorial, Sag Harbor, New York

2006

   British Consulate, New York, Retrospective

   Dahesh Museum, New York, Trustees Tour of the Artist's Studio

   Kips Bay Boys & Girls Club, *Designer Showcase*, New York

   School of Visual Arts, New York, *William Blake Influences*

   Art for Youth, London

2005

   Paul Labrecque Salons, New York

   Walter Wickiser Gallery, New York

2004

   Oxford University, Oxford, United Kingdom

2003

   Asia Society and Museum, New York

2002

   Art for Healing Gallery, New York

1999

Southampton College, Southampton, New York

1996

Film Center's Step-Daughter, The Salon Des Artistes, New York
Night Angel, musical, Clark Theater, Lincoln Center, New York

1994

Boat Child, National Theatre Conservatory, Denver

1993–1997

The Art of Love
   Civic Fine Arts Center, Sioux Falls, South Dakota
   The Embassy of France, Washington, DC
   The Foothills Art Center, Golden, Colorado
   The French Cultural Embassy, New York
   The French Library in Boston
   L'Alliance Française de New Orleans
   L'Alliance Française de Miami
   L'Alliance Française de San Francisco
   L'Alliance Française de Houston
   L'Alliance Française de Chicago
   Lincoln Center, New York
   The Nicolaysen Art Museum, Casper, Wyoming
   The West Hartford Art League, West Hartford, Connecticut

SERIES OF ARTWORKS

Adolescence, 1966

Arenal Volcan, 2004

The Art of Love, 1992

Badlands, 1988

Barcelona Point, 1992

Birthing, 1998

Bliss, 2008

Caves of Chauvet, 2005

Childhood, 1965

Children, 1981

China, 1985

Déclarations D'Amour, 1975

Earthly Fidelity, 1996

Frank, 1986

Horses of Chauvet, 2005

Icons, 2005

Living in Lightness and Darkness, 2008

Luminous Bodies, 1995

Mother & Child, 1988

Mummy Book, 1998

Night Angel, 1995

Playa Manuel Antonio, 2008

Queen, 1960

Recuperation, 2007

Return to Earth and Fire, 2008

Self-Portraits, 1982

Triptychs, 2000

Waves and Particles, 2008

Wedding, 1985

LITERATURE

NON-FICTION

Through Parisian Eyes: Reflections on Contemporary French Arts and
Culture, 1986, Oxford University Press, New York

Olhar Parisiense, Reflexoes Sobre a Cultue e as Artes Francesas
Contemporaneas, Portugese, 1991, Rio Fundo Editora, Ltda

NOVELS

Badlands, 1996

Child of the Western World, 1982

Floating Boundaries, A Trilogy, 1985

    Book I: Hong Kong

    Book II: China Arrives

    Book III: Freedom or Tyranny

Frank, 1996

Imogen, 1987

The Male Madonna, 1987

Rachel, 1980

PLAYS

Boat Child, a comedy, 1993

Caves of Chauvet, a musical, 2004

Horses of Chauvet, a musical, 2003

Journey to Benares, a musical, score by Elizabeth Swados, 2004

More Verse More, 1979

Night Angel, a musical, score by Carman Moore, 1992

Night Angel, a musical, score by Keith Bright, 1994

The Interviewer, a drama, 1981

SHORT STORIES

Outline for a Novel, 1984

The Photographer's Shoot, 1983

Poetry Volumes

Ancestors, 2006

The Art of Love: Love Poems and Paintings, 1990

Déclarations D'Amours, 1998 (French)

Early Years, 1970

Earthly Fidelity, 1997

Emotions, 1970

Expanse of Oceans & Seas, 2008

Finding Love, 1980

Gardens of Life, 2008

Healing, 2007

Human Conflicts, 2003

Illness, 2007

The Interviewer, 1982

Into the Waves, 2008

Love Brings Conflicts, 1976

Luminous Bodies, 1995

Post Traumatic Stress Syndrome, 2007

The Ritual:Volume I, 1975

The Ritual: Volume II, 1980

For Robert & James, 2000

Rules for a Ritual, 1976

Where is God, 2008

Women Embraced, 1980

Women and Horses, 2005

Would I Break Open My Heart Again, 1978

FILM

The Art of Love, 1993

Joyce Beroneo on Photography, 1983

The Kitchen, 1977

La Mort O'elle, 1976

Luminous Journey, 1999

Sacred Journey, 2001

SCREENPLAYS

I'll Get Bye, 1981

Julian and Juliet, 1978

Michael: The Life and Works of Michael Apted

The Third Half, 1993

Time to Heal, 2007

PHOTOGRAPHY

Badlands, 1991

China, 1985

Genesis, 1978

Polaroid Self-Portraits, 1981

Journalism

Philippe Adrien, French Dramatist, Paris, 1977

Lyudmila Alexeyeva, Russian Human Rights Activist, New York, 1992 (with audio)

Laurie Anderson, American Singer, New York, 1983

Anthony Andrews, English Actor, Under the Volcano, Mexico, 1984 (with audio)

Jean Anouilh, French Dramatist, Lausanne, Switzerland, 1976

Michelangelo Antonioni, Italian Filmmaker, Rome, 1977

Michael Apted, English Filmmaker, NY, CA, London, 1999 (with audio & video)

Jean-Paul Aron, French Writer, Paris, 1976 (with audio)

David Bailey, British Photographer, Oxford, United Kingdom, 1973

Jean-Louis Barrault, French Dramatist, Paris 1978 (with audio)

Saul Bellow, American Writer, Nobel Prize in Literature
    Chicago, 1991 (with audio)

Ingmar Bergman, Swedish Filmmaker, Munich, 1977

Bernardo Bertolucci, Italian Filmmaker, Rome, 1979

Jacqueline Bissett, American Actress, Mexico, 1984 (with audio)

Walerian Borowczyk, Polish Filmmaker, Paris, 1975

Breyten Breytenbach, South African Writer, Paris, 1985 (with audio)

Peter Brook, English Dramatist, Paris, 1975 (with audio)

David Byrne, American Musician, New York, 1983 (with audio)

Marcel Carné, French Filmmaker, Paris, 1978

L. M. Kit Carson, American Actor, Paris, Texas, 1983 (with audio)

John Cassavetes, American Film Director, New York, 1984 (with audio)

Patrice Chéreau, French Film and Theater Director, Paris, 1975

Costa-Gavras, Greek Film Director, Paris, 1985 (with audio)

Liliana Cavani, Italian Filmmaker, Rome, 1977

Cyril Connolly, British Writer and Critic, Oxford, United Kingdom, 1971

Robert M. Crunden, American Cultural Historian, 1998

Régis Debray, French Writer, Paris 1985 (with audio)

Joan Didion, American Writer, New York 1993 (with audio)

Marguerite Duras, French Filmmaker and Writer, Paris, 1975

Jean Eustache, French Filmmaker, Paris, 1975

Federico Fellini, Italian Filmmaker, Rome, 1977

Albert Finney, English Actor, Mexico, 1984 (with audio)

Michael Fitzgerald, American Film Producer, Mexico, 1984 (with audio)

J. Hubert Francis, Mi'kmaq Musician and Spiritual Elder
     Big Cove, New Brunswick, Canada, 2001 (with video)

Guy Gallo, American Writer, Mexico, 1983 (with audio)

Françoise Giroud, French Journalist, Politician and Writer
     Paris, 1985 (with audio)

Nadine Gordimer, South African Writer, New York, 1994

Günter Grass, Artist and Writer, Nobel Prize in Literature
     New York, 1993 (with audio)

Peggy Guggenheim, Art Collector, Paris, 1975

Michael Hastings, British Playwright, Paris, 1976

John Huston, American Filmmaker, Mexico, 1984 (with audio)

Eugène Ionesco, Romanian Playwright, Oxford, UK, 1974

Edmond Jabès, Egyptian Poet and Writer, Paris, 1985

Ruth Prawer Jhabvala, Indian Writer, Paris, 1978

Pierre Klossowski, French Artist and Writer, Paris, 1975

Bernard Kouchner, Founder of Doctors Without Borders
     French Prime Minister, Paris, 1985 (with audio)

Akira Kurosawa, Japanese Filmmaker, New York, 1985 (with audio)

Bernard-Henri Lévy, French Filmmaker, Paris, 1985 (with audio)

Roy Lichtenstein, American Artist, New York, 1983 (with audio)

Michael Lonsdale, French Actor, Paris, 1985

Louis Malle, French Filmmaker, Paris, 1975 (with audio)

André Malraux, French Writer, Paris, 1975

Florence Malraux, Daughter of André Malraux, Paris, 1985

Peter Matthiessen, American Writer, New York, 1991 (with audio)

Juan Mendez, Argentinean Human Rights Activist, New York, 1993 (with audio)

Eugenio Montale, Italian Journalist and Poet
     Nobel Prize in Literature, Milan, Italy, 1976

Yves Montand, French Actor and Singer, Paris, 1985 (with audio)

Aryeh Neier, American Human Rights Activist, New York, 1993 (with audio)

Journalism Cont'd

Mike Nichols, American Film and Theater Director, New York, 1999 (with audio)

Joyce Carol Oates, American Writer, Princeton, New Jersey, 1993 (with audio)

Marcel Ophüls, French Filmmaker, Paris, 1977 (with audio)

Nagisa Oshima, Japanese Filmmaker, New York, 1991 (with audio)

Alan Parker, English Film Director, Wildwood, New Jersey, 1984 (with audio)

Octavio Paz, Mexican Writer, Nobel Prize in Literature, Mexico, 1982 (with audio)

Tom Phillips, British Artist and Historian, Paris, 1975

Jérôme Peignot, French Writer, Paris, 1975

Michael H. Posner, American Human Rights Activist, New York, 1993 (with audio)

Ishmael Reed, American Poet and Writer, New York, 1992 (with audio)

Alain Resnais, French Film Director, Paris ,1985 (with audio)

Jean-François Revel, French Journalist and Writer, Paris, 1985 (with audio)

Alain Robbe-Grillet, French Filmmaker and Writer, Paris, 1974

Éric Rohmer, French Filmmaker and Writer, Paris, 1975

Françoise Sagan, French Writer, Paris, 1978 (with audio)

Jean-Paul Sartre, French Philosopher and Writer, Paris, 1977

John Sayles, American Filmmaker, New York, 1991 (with audio)

Martin Scorsese, American Filmmaker, New York, 1998 (with audio)

Stuart Seide, American Theater Director, Paris, 1975

Delphine Seyrig, French Actress and Director, 1975

George Steiner, French-born American Philosopher and Writer
    Oxford, United Kingdom, 1973

Bertrand Tavernier, French Filmmaker, Paris, 1985 (with audio)

Olivier Todd, French Journalist and Writer, Paris, 1978 (with audio)

Peter Trippi, American Art Historian, New York, 2006 (with audio and video)

François Truffaut, French Filmmaker, Paris, 1975

Roger Vadim, French Filmmaker, Paris, 1975

Michel Veuthey, Swiss Human Rights Activist, New York, 1994 (with audio)

Jon Voight, American Actor, New York, 1987 (with audio)

Francis Warner, English Dramatist, Oxford, United Kingdom, 1977

Wim Wenders, German Filmmaker, Paris, Texas, 1983 (with audio)

Monique Wittig, French Author and Feminist, Paris, 1976

George Wolf, American Theater, New York, 1993 (with audio)

Susannah York, English Actress, New York, 1991 (with audio)

PRAISE

"Porter's and Blake's works ...the very essence of all great art."

—Robin Hamlyn

"...most pertinent to Camber Porter is Michelangelo."

—Peter Trippi

"Porter skillfully picks and chooses from the entire range of modernism."

—Nancy Karlins

"Sensuality is at the heart of Porter's work."

—The New York Times

"Porter, who is Redon's equal and, with effort, outsurpasser."

—Jeffrey Paine

"Few artists have the rigorously philosophical instincts."

—Leo Castelli

"Porter's willingness to listen well and challenge when necessary."

—Philadelphia Inquirer

"...sections remind me of Shaw and Wilde."

—Peter Perhonis

"Painter-Novelist...a line between erotic and obscene."

—The New York Times

"The great 'meltdown' of modern sexual anarchy."

—Saul Bellow

"*Frank* is a pleasure in every way."

—Mike Nichols

"*Badlands* is a very strong, very intelligent."

—Joyce Carol Oates

"…her vision is lyrical, yet unflinching."

—Peter Matthiessen

"…like a fierce poem, with a devastating effect on our self-esteem."

—Louis Malle

"An uneasy dream of sex and death and abandonment."

—Joan Didion

"…is a particularly readable and brilliantly compiled collection."

—Boston Sunday Globe

"…It is an exquisite prose poem."

—Michael Hastings

"*Through Parisian Eyes* is like a daylong trip to the candy store."

—San Francisco Chronicle

"Porter's poetry and paintings have a soft, lyrical quality."

—Ishmael Reed

"Porter so powerfully conjures is a place where wounds don't heal."

—Donna Seaman

"…she had a protean talent, a beautiful imagination and the energy
and courage to explore every avenue of art as far as it would take her."

—Robert Redford

Obituaries of Melinda Camber Porter

East Hampton Star, East Hampton, New York.

Lady Margaret Hall, Oxford University, Oxford, England, United Kingdom.

New York Women in Film & Television, New York, New York.

The Sag Harbor Express, Sag Harbor, New York.

Southampton Press, Southampton, New York.

The Times, London, England, United Kingdom.

For More Information from
Blake Press and the Melinda Camber Porter Archive:

melinda@melindacamberporter.com

www.MelindaCamberPorter.com

http://en.wikipedia.org/wiki/Melinda_Camber_Porter

www.cultureunplugged.com/storyteller/Joseph_Flicek

www.amazon.com/Melinda-Camber-Porter/e/B001HQ1BS6

Index

CPSIA information can be obtained
at www.ICGtesting.com
Printed in the USA
LVOW05*1218140317

527136LV00016B/70/P